EARTH'S CYCLES

The Rock Cycle

CHERYL JAKAB

A⁺

Smart Apple Media

This edition first published in 2008 in the United States of America by Smart Apple Media.

Smart Apple Media
2140 Howard Drive West
North Mankato, Minnesota 56003

First published in 2007 by
MACMILLAN EDUCATION AUSTRALIA PTY LTD
627 Chapel Street, South Yarra, Australia 3141

Visit our Web site at www.macmillan.com.au or go directly to www.macmillanlibrary.com.au

Associated companies and representatives throughout the world.

Library of Congress Cataloging-in-Publication Data

Jakab, Cheryl.
    The rock cycle / by Cheryl Jakab.
    p. cm. — (Earth's cycles)
    Includes index.
    ISBN 978-1-59920-145-0
    1. Petrology. 2. Geochemical cycles. I. Title.

QE431.2.J35 2007
552—dc22

2007004551

Edited by Erin Richards
Text and cover design by Christine Deering
Page layout by Christine Deering
Photo research by Jes Senbergs
Illustrations by Ann Likhovetsky, pp. 6, 11, 15, 17, 19; Paul Könye, p. 29.

Printed in U.S.

Acknowledgements
The author and the publisher are grateful to the following for permission to reproduce copyright material:

Front cover photographs: volcano erupting (center), courtesy of Photodisc; rocky landscape (background), courtesy of Photodisc.

AGStockUSA/Alamy, Inc., p. 27; Gary Crabbe/Alamy, p. 14; Tim Graham/Alamy, p. 25; Holt Studios International Ltd/Alamy, p. 23 (bottom); The National Trust Photolibrary/Alamy, p. 7; Photofusion Picture Library/Alamy, p. 26; Jon Barter/Auscape, p. 12 (right); Herve Berthoule/Auscape, p. 6; Oxford Scientific Films/Auscape, p. 5; Corbis, pp. 4 (middle right & top left), 20 (middle right & middle left); Rob Cruse, p. 28 (top); Dave Hamman/ Getty, p. 13 (top right); Lanz von Horsten/Getty, p. 15; John Lund/Getty, p. 22 (top); Paul Souders/Getty, p. 10 (bottom); Lonely Planet Images/ Ralph Lee Hopkins, p. 23 (top); iStockphoto.com, p. 11; Brian Downs/Lochman Transparencies, p. 21 (top); Jiri Lochman/Lochman Transparencies, pp.12 (left), 21 (bottom); Dennis Sarson/ Lochman Transparencies, p. 13 (top left); Darlene Shepherd/Lochman Transparencies, p. 28 (bottom); Natural Sciences Image Library (NSIL), p. 13 (bottom left & bottom right), 18; NASA, pp. 4 (center), 30; Photodisc, pp. 1, 4 (bottom left, bottom right, middle left & top right), 8, 10 (top), 20 (bottom left, bottom right, center & top), 24; Photolibrary, pp. 9, 16; J&E Richards, p. 22 (bottom).

Contents

Volcanic rock

Metamorphic rock

Sand and sediment

Sedimentary rock

ideas and tips

Glossary words
When a word is printed
in **bold**, you can look
up its meaning in the
glossary on page 31.

Earth's natural cycles

What is a cycle?

A cycle is a never-ending series of changes that repeats again and again. Arrows in cycle diagrams show the direction in which the cycle is moving.

Earth's natural cycles create every environment on Earth. Living and non-living things are constantly changing. Each change is part of a natural cycle Earth's natural cycles are working all the time

Earth's non-living cycles are:
- the water cycle
- the rock cycle
- the seasons cycle

Earth's living cycles are:
- the food cycle
- the animal life cycle
- the plant life cycle

Earth's natural cycles keep the planet healthy.

4

The balance of nature

Earth's natural cycles all connect with each other. The way the cycles connect is sometimes called the balance of nature.

Keeping the balance

Every living thing depends on Earth's natural cycles to survive. A change in one cycle can affect the whole balance of nature. Knowing how Earth's cycles work helps us keep the environment healthy.

Every living thing depends on the balance of nature to survive.

Rocks

What are rocks?

Rocks are lumps of hard crystal material, made up of non-living **minerals**. A grain of sand is a small rock of just one mineral crystal. A large rock, such as a granite boulder, is made of a very large number of crystals in one hard lump.

Rocks make up the hard surface layer of Earth, called the crust. Rocks form all the features of the land, such as mountains, river valleys, coastlines, and the ocean bottom. Rocks are solid, but they are constantly changing.

Rocks are made of mineral crystals.

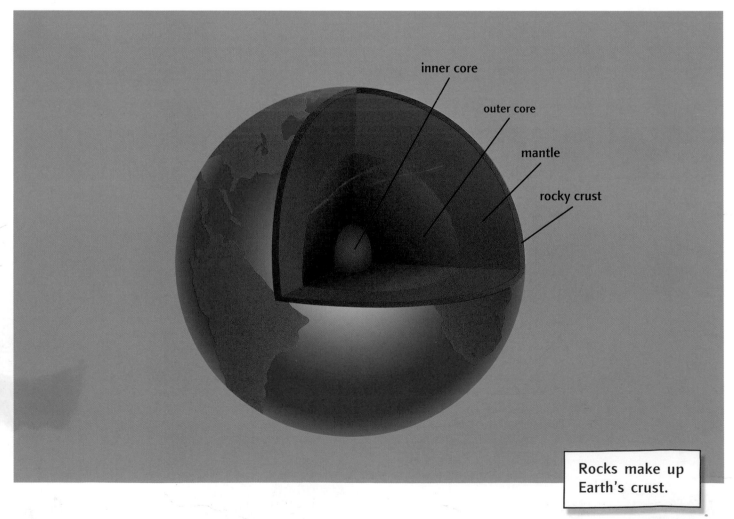

inner core

outer core

mantle

rocky crust

Rocks make up Earth's crust.

6

The importance of rocks

Rocks and soil are a very important part of the natural environment. They form the surface of the land.

Why are rocks important to people?

People need rocks and soil to grow food and for building. Many **resources** come from rocks and soil and are used by people every day.

How do people affect rocks and soil?

People affect rocks and soil when they mine the land for coal, oil, metals and other resources. Clearing the land for farms and towns can also cause **erosion**.

How do rocks fit into the balance of nature?

Rocks and soil form the surface of the land and the bottom of the oceans. They are the base of every habitat. Soil provides **nutrients** for plants and animals to grow.

Rocks and soil form the land.

7

The rock cycle

The rock cycle shows how different rocks form over time. Volcanic rock, sand and sediments, sedimentary rock, and metamorphic rock are all stages of the rock cycle. Rocks moving through the rock cycle renew the surface of Earth.

Volcanic rock

Sand and sediment

Metamorphic rock

Sedimentary rock

Rocks change from one type to another as they move through the rock cycle.

Moving through the rock cycle

Rocks move through the rock cycle in different ways. Not every rock follows the same pathway. A rock blasted from a volcano might stay on Earth's surface for millions of years and break down slowly. Another rock blasted from a volcano might go straight back under the surface and melt.

This rock formation in Ireland has stayed unchanged on Earth's surface for millions of years.

Volcanic rock

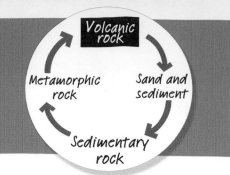

New volcanic rock is formed from **lava** or **magma** in this stage of the rock cycle. Lava is the name given to melted rock on Earth's surface. When it is below the surface, it is called magma. Volcanic rocks form when magma erupts from a volcano. The hot liquid lava cools quickly on the surface. As it cools, it hardens into solid rock. Different types of lava have different minerals in them, and form different types of volcanic rock.

Volcanic eruptions blast lava onto Earth's surface.

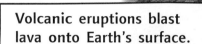
Lava cools on the surface to form volcanic rock.

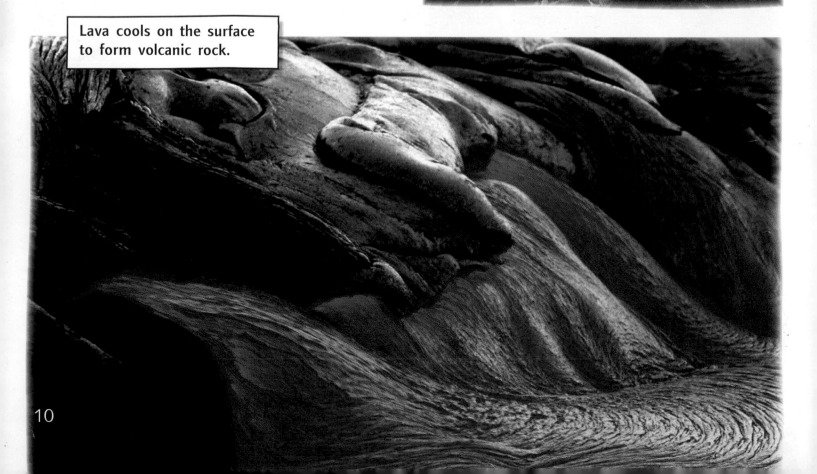

Slow-cooling magma

Magma can cool to form solid rock while still underground, as well as erupting from a volcano. Rocks that have cooled under the surface are only seen when the surrounding soil erodes away. They can also be seen when sudden events, such as earthquakes, lift them to the surface.

Soil has worn away over time, exposing this volcanic rock in Brazil.

lava

slow-cooling magma

magma

Volcanic rock can form underground or on Earth's surface.

11

Sand and sediment

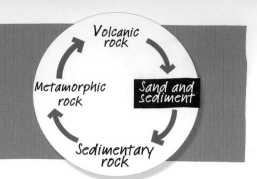

In the next stage of the rock cycle, rocks on Earth's surface are slowly worn down to become sand and sediments. Wearing rocks down into smaller pieces is called **weathering**. The main causes of weathering are wind and water. Winds blow against rocks, waves crash against them, and rivers flow over them. It can take many thousands of years for a rock exposed to weathering to break down into sediment.

Wind and water weathered this rock, causing it to crumble.

Parent rocks and sediment

Sediment is weathered from rocks called parent rocks. Every type of rock can be weathered into tiny pieces. Sediment can be large, small, hard, or soft. The type of sediment formed depends on the parent rock it came from. Quartz is the parent rock of sand. Feldspar is the parent rock of clay.

Parent rock

Sediment

Quartz rock will eventually weather into sand.

Parent rock

Sediment

Feldspar will eventually weather into clay.

Sedimentary rock

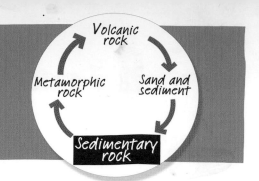

The next stage of the rock cycle is layers of sediment being pressed together to form sedimentary rock. This stage occurs after large amounts of sediment, weathered from rocks, are carried and dropped by wind and water. Fast-flowing rivers carry sediment downstream. As it slows down, sediment sinks to the bottom of the river as deposits. Thick sedimentary layers build up slowly over millions of years.

Layers can often be seen in sedimentary rock.

Forming sedimentary rock

Sedimentary rock often forms under water. Sediment collects at river mouths, in shallow lakes and seas, and on the ocean floor. Plant and animal material can add to sediments. As thick sedimentary layers build up, the weight of the top layers presses the lower layers into solid rock.

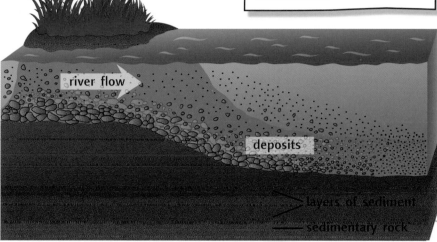

Large amounts of sediment are deposited by a river before small sediments.

river flow

deposits

layers of sediment

sedimentary rock

Types of sedimentary rock

Different types of sediment form different types of sedimentary rock. Sandstone is made from grains of sand weathered from older rocks. The sand is cemented together and hardened by pressure to form new rock. Silt and clay form a rock called shale. Limestone·is formed of the shells of tiny animals that lived long ago. Coal is the remains of plants that lived long ago.

Sand on this coastline may one day form sedimentary rock.

Metamorphic rock

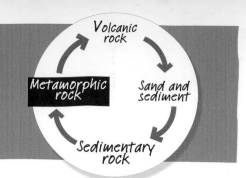

In the next stage of the rock cycle, volcanic and sedimentary rocks change form to become metamorphic rocks. Metamorphic rock gets its name from the Greek words "meta," meaning "change," and "morph," meaning "form." Rocks can be changed, or metamorphosed, by heat and pressure deep under Earth's surface. Even metamorphic rocks can be changed to form another type of metamorphic rock.

This metamorphic rock was folded by the movement of Earth's crust.

Heat and pressure

Below Earth's crust, extreme heat and pressure can melt rocks. Some rocks do not melt, but the crystals inside them change, forming metamorphic rocks. Heat from deep inside Earth can "bake" a rock and change its form. Limestone can be metamorphosed in this way to become marble. Shale is metamorphosed by intense heat and pressure to form slate.

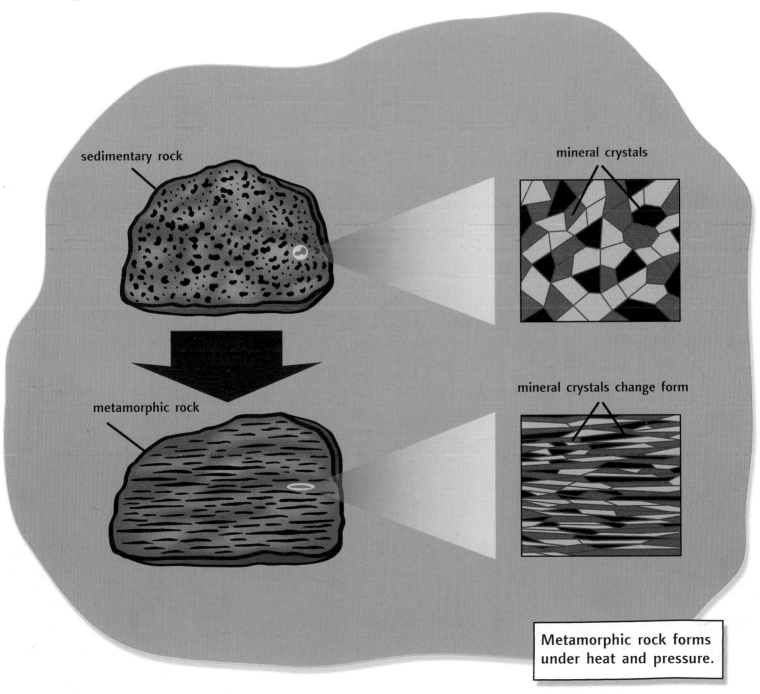

sedimentary rock

mineral crystals

metamorphic rock

mineral crystals change form

Metamorphic rock forms under heat and pressure.

Soil

What is soil?

Soil is the thin soft layer covering most of Earth's surface. Rock sediment makes up the main part of soil.

The weathered surface layer of Earth's crust has a very thin covering, called soil. Soil occurs in three main layers. They are topsoil, subsoil, and parent rock. The upper layer, or topsoil, is the most **fertile** layer of soil. It provides minerals and nutrients for plants and some animals to grow and live.

topsoil

subsoil

parent rock

Soil occurs in three main layers.

18

How soil forms

Soil forms when sand and other rock sediment combines with rotting plant and animal material, called **humus**. Sediment on the surface changes slowly into soil due to the actions of **decomposers**, such as fungi, worms, and **bacteria**. Large sediment forms sandy soil. Fine sediment forms clay soil. Most good soil includes large and small sediment.

Soil forms very slowly over many years.

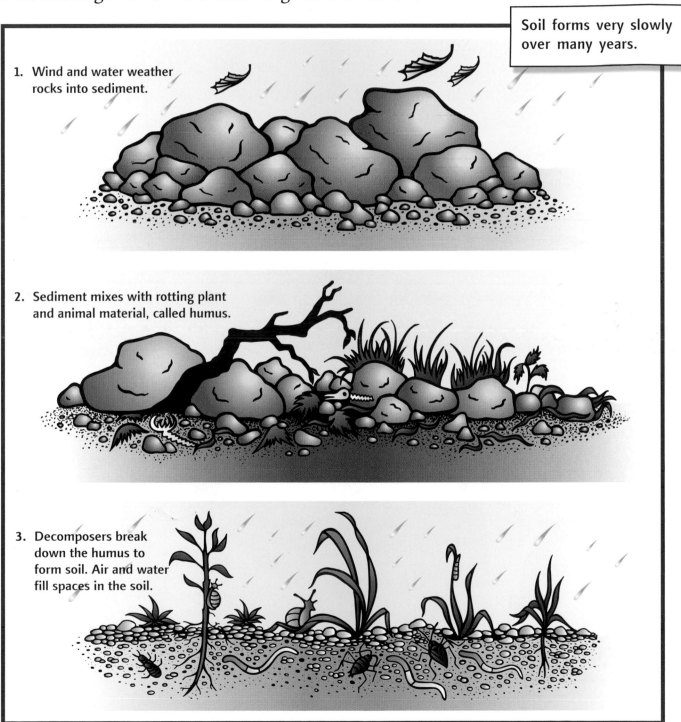

1. Wind and water weather rocks into sediment.

2. Sediment mixes with rotting plant and animal material, called humus.

3. Decomposers break down the humus to form soil. Air and water fill spaces in the soil.

The balance of nature

The balance of nature shows how the rock cycle is linked with Earth's other cycles. Rocks have an effect on non-living and living things in every environment on Earth. The seasons, food, water, plants, and animals all help to maintain the rock cycle.

Food cycle

Seasons cycle

Rock cycle

Plant life cycle

Water cycle

Animal life cycle

The rock cycle is an important part of the balance of nature.

Rocks and seasons

The changing seasons bring different temperatures, rainfall, and winds to Earth's surface. Rocks are weathered by rain and wind. Repeated changes of temperature from hot to cold can break rocks apart.

Rocks and water

Rocks are weathered by moving water. How fast they weather depends on the hardness of the rock. It also depends on the amount of water and how fast the water is moving. Material carried in the water, such as sediment, also helps to weather rocks.

A change in temperature can cause a rock to split.

Ocean waves have weathered this rock to create a blowhole.

Herds of animals can cause soil erosion.

Rocks, soil, and animals

Many animals build their homes and nests in rocks and soil. The remains of dead animals combine with rock sediment to form soil. As animals move over land they can cause rocks and soil to erode.

Rocks and plants

The remains of dead plants combine with sediment to form soil. Plants grow with their roots in the soil, which helps hold soils together. Plant roots can also break up large rocks by pushing through cracks in the rocks.

Tree roots work their way through cracks in the rocks at this temple in Cambodia.

Rocks, soil, and food

Rocks and soil play an important part in the food cycle. They provide plants with the minerals and nutrients they need to grow. Plants are food for people and animals. When plants and animals die, their bodies decompose, and the nutrients are recycled back into the soil.

Leaf litter on the forest floor rots away and returns nutrients to the soil.

Many foods grow in fertile soil.

23

People and rocks

People use rocks and soil in many different ways. This can affect the rock cycle. People can damage rocks and soil when they:

- mine the land without caring for the environment
- overuse mineral resources
- clear the land, causing topsoil to erode
- reduce the fertility of soil
- poison soil with insecticides and other chemicals

Strip-mining can damage the environment.

Mining

Many areas have been badly damaged by mining. Nauru, a small coral island in the Pacific Ocean, was rich in deposits of **phosphate rock**. Mining the phosphate removed the topsoil. This left 80 percent of the island with an environment that cannot sustain life. Learning from this experience can help us find more **sustainable** ways of using rocks and soil.

Most of the natural habitat on Nauru has been lost.

Using rocks and soil wisely

Using rocks and soil wisely can help keep the rock cycle working well. People help when they:

- mine carefully to limit land damage
- recycle mined resources
- prevent soil erosion by not cutting down trees
- plant trees to stop soil erosion
- use farming methods that make soil more fertile
- stop poisoning soil with insecticides

Replanting mined areas can help limit land damage.

Soil conservation

Soil conservation is the protection of soil. It includes any method that keeps soil fertile and prevents erosion. Soil is a very important resource on Earth. It takes a long time to form and, once eroded, is very hard to replace. People can use good farming methods to help save soil. Replanting cleared forests can make soil richer. Tree planting projects can also prevent and stop erosion.

Good farming practices help maintain healthy soil.

Saving rocks and soil

Everyone can help protect rocks and soil. Many valuable resources from rocks and soil are dumped as garbage. Reducing garbage, recycling, and reusing resources can help save rocks and soil.

Reduce garbage

- Buy food with less packaging
- Say "no" to plastic shopping bags
- Turn vegetable scraps into compost

Recycle and reuse

- Recycle glass and metals, reducing the need to mine the land
- Recycle paper, reducing the need to cut down trees
- Reuse glass bottles and plastic containers at home
- Take lunch to school in a reusable lunch box

Leaf litter can be added to compost.

Recycling reduces the need to mine for raw materials.

Compost project

Start a compost bin to help make the soil in your garden richer. Find out what should go in the compost bin by placing small pieces of food on some soil.

What you need

- one cardboard milk carton, cut in half lengthways
- six different scraps of food
- soil
- a spray bottle filled with water

What to do

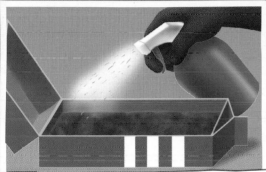

1 Fill one half of the milk carton with a layer of soil, about 1 inch (2cm) thick. Use the spray bottle to moisten the soil with water.

2 Place scraps of food on top of the soil. You could try apple cores, bits of cheese, bread crusts or orange peel.

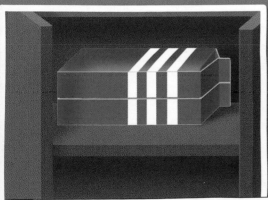

3 Cover the container with the other half of the milk carton. Keep the container in a cool, dark place.

4 Remove the cover each day and look at the food scraps. Are some foods rotting faster than others?

Which foods make good compost?

Living with nature

We all depend on the balance of nature for our survival. If people continue to disturb Earth's cycles, it will upset the balance of nature. Understanding Earth's cycles helps us care for Earth and live in harmony with nature.

"The Earth does not belong to us: we belong to the Earth."

(Chief Seattle Suquamish leader, about 1854)

Glossary

bacteria	microscopic decomposers
decomposers	living things that break down dead plant and animal material
erosion	the wearing away of rocks and soil
fertile	rich in minerals and nutrients needed for plant growth
humus	decomposed plant and animal material
lava	hot liquid rock on Earth's surface
magma	hot liquid rock underground
minerals	non-living substances found in rocks and soil
nutrients	substances that give living things energy
phosphate rock	rock made of phosphate minerals, used by people to make fertilizer
resources	materials considered to be valuable or useful
sustainable	able to be continued without damaging the environment
weathering	the wearing down of rocks into smaller pieces

Index